VOICES UNHEARD

PRACTICAL INSIGHTS FOR DEEPENING UNDERSTANDING AND CREATING LASTING CHANGE

AN EQUITY, DIVERSITY, AND INCLUSION SUCCESS GUIDE

LENA IMADA

Copyright © 2024 by Lena Imada

All rights reserved. No part of this book may be reproduced, distributed, or transmitted in any form or by any means, including photocopying, recording, or other electronic or mechanical methods, without the prior written permission of the publisher, except in the case of brief quotations embodied in critical reviews and certain other noncommercial uses permitted by copyright law. For permission requests, write to the publisher at the address below:

Publisher's Contact Information: Lena Imada, lenaimada@hotmail.com

This book is a work of nonfiction. The events and experiences described are based on the author's recollections and insights.

Cover and Layout by Hmdpublishing

Narration by: Lena Imada

ISBN: 9798344095172

First Edition: October, 2024

Disclaimer

The content in this book is based on my personal experiences, reflections, and research. I have taken great care to analyze my thoughts objectively and present them without being influenced by emotions. My aim is to foster understanding, encourage growth, and provide insights supported by evidence wherever possible. However, I acknowledge that some readers may not agree with everything written here, and that's okay.

If you find yourself disagreeing with certain points or feeling uncomfortable with some ideas, I encourage you to pause and reflect on why that is. Challenge yourself to question the source of your perspective, examine any underlying assumptions, and consider how your own experiences might be shaping your views. I also suggest conducting additional research to deepen your understanding of the topics presented.

While I have made every effort to protect the privacy of individuals by omitting specific names and identities from my personal stories, some readers may recognize certain events or situations. I want to emphasize that this book is not intended to hurt or attack anyone. I do not hold any blame toward those whose actions or words have been part of my experiences. I fully recognize that these actions were likely not intended to harm, but rather are reflective of unconscious biases and a lack of awareness. My intention is purely educational—to encourage all of us to become more mindful and aware of how our behaviors can impact others.

We all have different perceptions shaped by our unique backgrounds, and even when we strive to remove biases, our interpretations can still vary. The goal of this book is not to convince you to adopt a single point of view, but rather to inspire you to practice deep self-reflection and engage with these issues thoughtfully. By doing so, we can collectively move toward creating an environment that is respectful, inclusive, and truly welcoming for everyone.

Thank you for being open to this journey. I hope that what you find here sparks meaningful conversations and a deeper commitment to equity, diversity, and inclusion.

"To everyone who bravely stands up for Equity, Diversity, and Inclusion—not just for your own well-being, but for the future of those who will follow: Your courage, persistence, and unwavering commitment do not go unnoticed. This book is a tribute to your work, and I hope it serves as a reminder that your advocacy is both vital and powerful. A special thank you to Atsuko, Susana, and my EDI Committee colleagues. You cared, listened, validated my concerns, and gave me the strength to keep going each day. I would also like to acknowledge those who have profoundly impacted my life: Parul, Reza, Hamid, Imelda, Laleh, Lisa, Ahmed, Mona, Mina, and RJ, just to name a few. Your kindness, hard work, bravery, and relentless efforts to thrive in a new country have been a true source of inspiration. I've witnessed your struggles and successes, and I know how challenging the journey has been. I hold immense respect for each of you. To my long-time friends who are more like sisters—Lilla, Regine, and Erin: Your unwavering support and genuine friendship have meant everything to me. Through countless hours of listening and being there during my toughest moments, I am forever grateful. I also want to extend a heartfelt thank you to Melissa, Marla, Noor, Mary-Jane, Tamara, and Derushka for their friendship, for validating my struggles, and for offering your support when I needed it the most. To anyone else who has cared for me, listened to my struggles, and supported me along the way—your kindness has not gone unnoticed, and I am deeply grateful. Lastly, my deepest gratitude goes to my family, especially my husband, who has been my rock through the most challenging years. Your love and support have been my foundation and given me the strength to persevere. I feel truly blessed to have you all in my life."

CONTENTS

CHAPTER 01.
INTRODUCTION TO EQUITY, DIVERSITY,
AND INCLUSION (EDI) – MY JOURNEY AS A MINORITY   5

CHAPTER 02.
WHY I WROTE THIS BOOK   15

CHAPTER 03.
THE HISTORY OF IMMIGRATION IN CANADA   25

CHAPTER 04.
UNDERSTANDING UNCONSCIOUS BIAS AND INSECURITY   29

CHAPTER 05.
SEEING THE WORLD AS A MINORITY   42

CHAPTER 06.
INDIGENOUS LAND ACKNOWLEDGEMENT:
A STEP TOWARD GENUINE REFLECTION   55

CHAPTER 07.
EMPOWERING CHANGE: TAKING THE FIRST STEP   59

REFERENCES 73

CHAPTER 01

INTRODUCTION TO EQUITY, DIVERSITY, AND INCLUSION (EDI) – MY JOURNEY AS A MINORITY

What do you think of when you hear the words Equity, Diversity, and Inclusion? Do you feel happy because you live in a community where diversity is celebrated, and everyone is treated equally? Or do you feel sad, angry, or emotional because of your own experiences as a minority being treated unfairly? Maybe you feel neutral, believing that EDI doesn't directly impact you because you fit into the majority category in your community. Regardless of your reaction, EDI is a fundamental part of creating spaces where every individual feels respected, valued, and empowered to thrive.

Equity, Diversity, and Inclusion (EDI) are concepts that, on the surface, may sound simple, but they carry profound implications. Equity means fairness—it's about ensuring everyone has access to the same opportunities by recognizing and addressing existing imbalances and barriers. Imagine you're handing out shoes: equity is not about giving everyone the same size, but rather ensuring everyone gets a pair that fits. Diversity is about variety—bringing different perspectives, backgrounds, and identities to the table. It's not just about race or gender but includes age, abilities, sexual orientation, and even life experiences. Finally, Inclusion means making sure those diverse voices are actively heard and valued. It's not just being invited to the party, but also being asked to dance. Together, EDI creates an environment where people can truly thrive, contribute, and feel a sense of belonging.

Understanding the Layers of Minority Identity

The term "minority" is not as simple as it might first appear. It carries with it many layers of complexity, extending beyond just race or ethnicity. As a minority myself, I've often struggled to understand why I was treated differently in certain situations. Was it because I'm a woman? Was it because I'm Asian? Was it my accent or the darker color of my skin? Each of these factors—gender, race, language, and appearance—has intersected at different times to shape my experiences in ways that left me feeling isolated or misunderstood.

But being a minority isn't a fixed identity—it's fluid and situational. I've been the only woman in a room full of men, or the only Japanese person in a group of other Asians, where I still felt like a minority. Similarly, a Caucasian person living in an Asian country may experience what it's like to be in the minority and face cultural or linguistic barriers. The concept of being a minority shifts depending on the environment, making it a universal experience that can touch anyone's life at different points. That's why understanding EDI is so important for everyone—it's not limited to traditionally marginalized groups. We can all find ourselves in situations where we are underrepresented or feel out of place.

When we recognize that minority status is not always tied to just one identity marker, we open ourselves to a deeper empathy for others' experiences and develop a stronger commitment to fostering inclusivity. Whether based on race, gender, or any other characteristic, the goal of EDI is to ensure that everyone feels valued and respected, regardless of their position in a group.

Why EDI Is Personal to Me

For me, EDI is not just a framework or checklist—it is a deeply personal and lived experience. My understanding of these concepts has been shaped through years of navigating different cultures, environments, and biases. Growing up, I stood up for those who were marginalized when people were treated unjustly. I realized early on that prejudice and exclusion often stem from ignorance and insecurity, rather than an individual's intrinsic worth.

A Childhood Lesson in Fairness: Standing Up for a Classmate

One of the most pivotal moments in my early understanding of fairness occurred in third grade, when a new student with severe atopic dermatitis joined our class. His skin condition made him the target of cruel remarks and exclusion because of his appearance and the strong smell of his medication. I remember watching this unfold, feeling a sense of confusion and frustration. Why should anyone be mistreated for something beyond their control?

One day, I couldn't stay silent any longer. I stood up for him in front of the class and asked, "Do you think he wanted to be born like this?" The room fell silent. My classmates were confronted with a truth they hadn't considered, and the boy's tormentor eventually apologized. That moment solidified my understanding of injustice and the importance of speaking up—values that would continue to shape my approach to EDI in the years to come. This experience taught me that true equity means creating environments where we recognize and address the unique struggles people face. Inclusion starts with empathy and the courage to stand against what feels "normal" when it perpetuates harm. While this may seem simple in theory, it requires a willingness to disrupt the status quo—a lesson I would carry forward into new, more challenging environments.

My Personal Journey and Why I Left Japan

As I entered my teenage years, I found myself increasingly captivated by Western culture, particularly through its music, movies, and literature. This exposure sparked a yearning to explore beyond the boundaries of my small hometown in Seto, Japan. I craved an environment where individuality was not just accepted but celebrated—a stark contrast to the highly conformist culture I was surrounded by. In Japan, there's a well-known saying that perfectly captures this societal expectation: *"The nail that sticks out gets hammered down."* Even as a child, I found this concept perplexing. Why should every nail be the same? I believed that each nail should have its own color, shape, and length, so that we could stand out in our own unique ways. If everyone embraced their differences, wouldn't the world be a richer, more vibrant place—one where creativity thrives, and no one has to conform just to avoid being "hammered down"?

That longing for personal freedom is what drove me to seek opportunities abroad. After discovering a student exchange program online—using a computer I had begged my father to buy me—I convinced my parents to let me study in the United States. I still remember the excitement I felt—this was my chance to step out of the familiar and into a world filled with different perspectives, cultures, and experiences.

The Emotional Toll: Alabama and Learning to Smile Through It

However, stepping into this new world wasn't as easy as I had imagined. When I arrived in Elba, Alabama—a small town where cultural and racial divisions were starkly visible—I was confronted with the emotional labor of navigating life as a minority. The high school was nearly evenly split between Caucasian and African American students, and I stood out as the only East Asian. The racial divide was most apparent in the lunchroom, where seating arrangements were segregated, and this separation extended into communities and churches outside of school. As a child, unaware of the historical context behind these divisions, I didn't fully understand why they existed—but I remember feeling a deep sadness over the barriers that kept people apart.

Without the language skills to communicate, I was anxious that people wouldn't like me or even talk to me—not just because I couldn't speak English well, but because I looked different. In my struggle to navigate this unfamiliar environment, I came up with a small coping mechanism: each morning, I would draw a smiley face on my palm as a reminder to stay positive, no matter what happened. I believed that if I kept smiling and made myself appear approachable, people couldn't hate me—and perhaps, they might even talk to me.

Even on the hardest days—like when I sensed people were laughing at me in a negative way as a group—I would glance at that tiny smiley face I had drawn on my palm, as if it were reminding me to stay positive and strong. It felt like a fragile lifeline, a small symbol of hope that encouraged me to push through the anxiety and keep trying to connect with others. Those months weren't just about learning English; they were about preserving my sense of self while navigating a divided community. I quickly realized that fitting in wasn't just a matter of speaking the same language—it required breaking through social and emotional barriers, often alone.

I was fortunate enough to meet a few people who saw me as just another human being beyond racial differences. Over time, as people got used to me, many seemed to realize that I wasn't all that different from them—I just looked a little different. This shift in perception, I believe, was largely due to unfamiliarity and stereotypes in a community where multiculturalism was virtually nonexistent. This experience showed me the importance of diverse representation in media—movies, music, TV shows, commercials, and magazines—because they shape how people perceive others from a young age. When people are exposed to diverse cultures and identities early on, it fosters an understanding that everyone is fundamentally the same, reducing racial biases and promoting inclusivity.

I've personally experienced the negative effects of this divide in representation when classmates in Alabama would mock the Chinese language in front of me or pull their eyelids back to imitate Asian eyes. While I understood that they didn't grasp the differences between Asian nationalities, it was disheartening to realize that they made sweeping assumptions based on stereotypes rather than making an effort to see me as an individual beyond those labels.

This is why representation matters—not just in media but in everyday life. Communities that lack diversity must consciously strive to educate themselves and their children about different cultures and people. Parents can play a pivotal role by encouraging regular discussions about various backgrounds, cultures, and identities at home. If children express stereotypes or assumptions, it's an opportunity to gently challenge these notions. Ask them to reflect on whether the statement is true or untrue, and explore why they may have formed that belief. By engaging in these conversations, we teach them to question biases and build the critical thinking skills necessary to form well-rounded, bias-free opinions in the future.

Ultimately, this practice fosters empathy and a deeper understanding of others, cultivating a generation better equipped to contribute to a world where everyone's unique identity is respected and celebrated. Such skills are invaluable—not just for building inclusive communities but for navigating a diverse and interconnected world.

One company that has been making strides in this area is Gap Inc. They have made diversity, equity, and inclusion central to their business strategy. Through initiatives like the Color Proud Council, launched in 2018, Gap Inc. focuses on ensuring that their product design, merchandising, and marketing reflect a wide range of skin tones, body sizes, and cultural backgrounds. This approach extends to their advertising, where they are committed to featuring diverse talent—both in front of and behind the camera. Currently, over 50% of the people represented in their advertising campaigns are people of color, and they are actively working to include underrepresented groups such as individuals with disabilities and members of the LGBTQ+ community (Gap Inc.).

Additionally, Gap Inc. has outlined ambitious goals for 2025, such as doubling the representation of Black and Latinx employees at all levels in their U.S. headquarters and increasing the representation of Black employees in store leadership roles by 50%. They are also actively collaborating with external partners to promote inclusion in the fashion industry and create opportunities for diverse designers and voices (Gap Inc.; Glossy).

Overall, companies like Gap Inc. are setting a positive example by using their platforms to challenge stereotypes and promote inclusivity, ensuring that people from all backgrounds see themselves represented in mainstream media. This type of visibility is crucial in shaping a world where no one feels marginalized because of their race, ethnicity, or identity. Had people grown up seeing Asians like me represented in positive and diverse roles, they might have viewed me as just another peer, rather than as a foreign curiosity. Unfortunately, stereotypes still shape perceptions, and I'm often confronted with the reminder that there's a significant lack of awareness.

My experience in Alabama reinforced that inclusion is not just about being present in a space, but about feeling seen and respected for who you are. True inclusion requires more than good intentions—it requires active effort and empathy. It was here, in a town divided along racial lines, that I began to understand how deeply societal structures shape our interactions. I learned that real inclusion means breaking down barriers that make people feel like they don't belong, whether those barriers are physical, cultural, or emotional.

Connecting Personal Experiences to the Broader EDI Landscape

In recent years, there has been an increase in EDI-related initiatives, and while this makes me hopeful, I worry that many organizations see them as boxes to tick rather than meaningful actions. Without a deep understanding of the significance of EDI, efforts can become hollow gestures. Whether you are an individual seeking to better understand EDI and gain insight into the minority experience, or a leader looking for practical tools to foster a more inclusive environment, I have included researched scenarios, relevant statistics, and thought-provoking exercises to support you on this journey.

Final Thoughts: Why EDI Matters for Everyone

EDI is about reshaping the environments we live and work in so that everyone has an equal opportunity to contribute and thrive. It's not just a set of organizational policies—it's a movement that begins with each of us. As you continue reading, I encourage you to reflect on your own experiences and consider: Whose voices are missing? What small actions can you take today to ensure that everyone feels seen, heard, and valued? Real change starts with these seemingly small, intentional choices.

REFLECTION EXERCISE:

Have you ever found yourself in a space where, despite being present, you felt invisible? What did that feel like? What would have made you feel more seen and included?

_____

_____

_____

_____

_____

_____

CHALLENGE YOURSELF:

Next time you notice someone being excluded or treated unfairly, ask yourself: *What small action can I take to create a more inclusive environment?* Whether it's offering support, inviting them to participate, or speaking up when it feels safe to do so, commit to taking one specific step to make others feel seen and valued. Write down this commitment and revisit it regularly to remind yourself to act when the opportunity arises.

CHAPTER 02
WHY I WROTE THIS BOOK

Despite the hope and energy I conveyed in Chapter 1, I've also encountered deep frustration. Although Equity, Diversity, and Inclusion (EDI) has been a focal point of discussion for years, genuine, systemic change often feels painstakingly slow. It's like Sisyphus pushing a boulder up a steep hill, only to watch it slide back down repeatedly. In this chapter, I'll delve into what motivated me to write this book and the source of the drive that keeps me moving forward, despite the setbacks.

1. Frustration with the Slow Pace of Change

Many people still can't relate to the lived experiences of minorities, and without that sense of understanding, there's no urgency to resolve these issues. I often feel as though the conversations around EDI are happening, but they lack the depth and action needed to create lasting change. Writing this book is my way of ensuring that my years of advocating and fighting for minorities weren't in vain. It's also a way to inspire others to recognize how crucial EDI is and to encourage them to take action, no matter how small.

I've witnessed the frustration this causes firsthand, not only in my own advocacy work but also through the experiences of friends who have been championing EDI for over 20 years. One colleague told me that she has only seen gradual change over the span of two decades—despite the countless hours of effort she has poured into the cause. Personally, I've joined multiple EDI groups over the past 10 years, and while we've dedicated so much energy and time, we often hit a wall within our organizations. Without active support from leaders, our impact is limited, and the changes we advocate for often fail to gain traction. It's disheartening to see momentum fizzle because the decision-makers aren't fully invested.

In the last five years or so, there has been a surge in conversations around EDI, and my friends and I feel an urgent need to maintain this momentum. More people are becoming familiar with the importance of these topics, and we don't want to lose this opportunity to create meaningful, lasting change. This book is my response to that urgency—a way to keep the conversation going and encourage everyone, from individuals to leaders, to recognize that the time to act is now.

2. Sharing Real-Life Stories to Educate Others

This frustration is precisely why I chose to share my story. If formal EDI strategies aren't driving change fast enough, then maybe personal stories can help bridge the gap and create understanding. Just as women have had to navigate a male-dominated system, minorities face similar struggles in being recognized and treated as equals. By sharing my own experiences, I hope to shed light on the subtle yet constant challenges that minorities face daily.

Throughout my journey, I gradually transitioned from calling out specific behaviors to a more educational approach, sharing personal stories to bridge understanding. This shift allowed me to engage others in conversations that I hoped would lead to meaningful reflection and change. However, this approach was not without its challenges. The more I spoke up, the more I felt that I was labeled as "difficult" or "opinionated," particularly when I questioned long-established systems. These labels, while frustrating, became a reminder of the resistance that often accompanies change. Though it was mentally exhausting at times, I learned to accept that pushing for equity often means making others uncomfortable.

Over time, I realized that directly confronting people often made them defensive. The more I framed my stories as opportunities to learn and grow together, the more willing people were to engage. It wasn't an easy change for me—there were moments when I doubted whether this gentler approach would work—but I noticed it opened up more space for dialogue. I began to see that making others uncomfortable wasn't just about pointing out flaws; it was about inviting them to step outside their comfort zones and truly listen. This became a turning point in my advocacy, shifting my focus from confrontation to collaboration.

3. Feeling Misunderstood and Labeled as Difficult

Throughout my career, I've encountered situations where my contributions were not fully understood or integrated into team discussions. When my perspectives diverged from the group consensus, they were often met with resistance. For instance, in one particular meeting, I raised a concern about being the only minority in our small team, which sometimes led to my viewpoints being unintentionally overlooked. Some of my colleagues, who shared similar backgrounds, often aligned in their problem-solving approaches. I suggested that this dynamic could be influencing our decisions, limiting the scope for broader perspectives.

Addressing this issue was challenging. I was mindful of not wanting to create the impression of being difficult or disruptive. My goal was to ensure my input was valued and that we could work together in a more inclusive environment. However, as my viewpoints often diverged from those of my colleagues, tension began to surface. In some cases, their responses seemed defensive, shifting the focus from collaboration to countering my input. This made it increasingly difficult to feel that my contributions were advancing the team's goals.

Over time, it became clear that some colleagues had already aligned on their positions before attending meetings. While I didn't believe this was done with any negative intent, it contributed to a sense of isolation. The experience became mentally exhausting, and I questioned whether my efforts were truly contributing to the team or being perceived as disruptive. As a result, I participated less frequently and gradually became disengaged. Despite my efforts to understand my colleagues' perspectives before offering my own, it was hard to feel fully understood. With limited feedback beyond my own perceptions to validate my observations, it felt as if I were navigating these dynamics alone.

Although my colleagues often assured me that all viewpoints were being taken into account, I continued to feel that my contributions were sidelined. This feeling was heightened by the lack of a cohesive team dynamic. In contrast to previous teams where I had felt genuinely valued, the absence of camaraderie only deepened my sense of isolation. I also feared that continuing to raise these issues might lead others to label me as difficult, a concern many minorities share in the workplace.

My colleagues often framed their responses as practical—suggesting that if a group of people felt confident in a solution, it made sense to go with the majority. While I understood their reasoning, this highlighted a broader issue: when the majority shares similar backgrounds, the perspective of a lone minority can be unintentionally sidelined. This wasn't necessarily about exclusion, but rather how familiarity can shape decision-making without conscious awareness. In our small team, this imbalance was particularly pronounced. I explained that it wasn't about blaming anyone but recognizing that without deliberate effort, familiar perspectives could dominate discussions. Despite my explanations, my input was sometimes overridden by a supervisor's decision to follow the majority view, which left me feeling unheard.

If I had felt that my input was genuinely welcomed and valued, and my colleagues had shown a willingness to collaborate and made efforts to understand my perspective, I know I would have approached these discussions with greater confidence. However, over time, it became clear that my viewpoints weren't being fully integrated into the decision-making process. This phenomenon—commonly referred to as "groupthink"—is a known challenge in homogeneous teams, where similar backgrounds and experiences often lead to a lack of diversity in thought (Janis, 1982). Without diversity, it becomes difficult to challenge assumptions or explore alternative perspectives, ultimately limiting innovation and problem-solving. Research supports the idea that people often gravitate toward familiar patterns of thinking, especially in group settings, unless they are consciously challenged to consider other viewpoints (Kahneman, 2011). While I don't fault my colleagues for this dynamic, it's important to recognize how easily unconscious biases can influence group decisions. It's not just about agreeing with the majority; it's about ensuring that all perspectives, especially those that differ, are given equal consideration.

I felt this became more evident when I attempted to escalate my concerns around the team dynamic. When I walked into the meeting to discuss those concerns, I quickly realized I was the only minority in a group of six others. Even though I knew they came with good intentions and were there to support me, the dynamic immediately made me feel uncomfortable and scared. I felt there was no one in the room who could truly relate to my experiences as a minority, and that terrified me, as I didn't know how I could validate my point without anyone who had faced similar challenges. Despite staying positive and approaching the meeting with an open mind, I soon realized I was facing barriers as a result of that composition. It felt as though I was walking into a losing battle, knowing I had to convince six members of the majority to validate my point of view. The situation felt intimidating, exhausting, and nearly impossible. In the end, very little changed, and I left feeling like I couldn't break through.

This echoed a similar experience early in my career when I became a Canadian citizen. Determined to be treated like everyone else, I didn't want any special treatment despite my accent or language limitations. When I was promoted, I sensed skepticism from my colleagues. One Caucasian woman, who had been assigned to train me in the new role, offered little help as I struggled to learn the job. When I asked for guidance, I was often met with reluctance. While I understood that everyone was busy, the stark difference in treatment between me and my new Caucasian colleagues was undeniable. I didn't blame her entirely—after all, we were all busy, and she wasn't being paid extra to train me. But it was hard. Every day, after everyone had gone home, I worked three extra hours, holding back tears but pushing through because I wanted to be good at my job and earn everyone's respect, especially hers.

While I was determined to stay positive and improve, I couldn't help but notice how differently I was treated compared to new Caucasian colleagues who joined the team. Their interactions with our coworkers seemed effortless—conversations flowed easily, and they were immediately accepted. I was the only one who struggled to break into these social circles. At one point, another minority woman joined our team, and it became painfully clear that exclusion wasn't just in my head. Both of us found ourselves isolated from the larger group. I made a conscious effort to join the team's conversations, going out with them after work to try and build rapport, but my colleague didn't. As a result, she was almost completely left out, which further highlighted the subtle, yet pervasive, dynamics of exclusion that existed.

Over the course of three months, I pushed myself relentlessly and finally reached a level where I could perform the job—perhaps not as well as my colleague, who had been there much longer, but well enough to keep up with her pace. Once I achieved that level of competence, her attitude toward me shifted. I felt as though she finally accepted me. But through this experience, and others that followed, I realized something important: no matter how much I improved or how hard I worked, I would always have to prove myself in new workplaces to gain the respect that others received from the start.

This ongoing challenge is known as the "prove it again" bias, where women and minorities must repeatedly demonstrate their competence to earn the same recognition as their peers (Williams et al., 2016). For visible minorities, this burden is compounded by other biases, like those linked to language and accent. Research by Lev-Ari and Keysar (2010) found that people often perceive speakers with accents as less credible, regardless of their actual expertise. This bias further diminishes opportunities for fair treatment and advancement, adding to the emotional labor and stress that minorities endure (Harris et al., 2018; Sue et al., 2007).

Looking back, I can't help but feel a deep sense of frustration and sadness. There seems to be no easy path for minorities to thrive in the same way as the majority. Like many others, I've considered staying silent, knowing that constantly speaking up often feels futile and exhausting. The hardest part of standing up for this issue is that I hate being misunderstood and labeled as difficult because I see myself as the complete opposite of difficult. I hate giving people a hard time or feeling like I'm causing unnecessary trouble. Despite this, I firmly believe that without genuine diversity in teams, and with decisions continually leaning toward the majority perspective, my voice—and the voices of other minorities—will remain marginalized. This only reinforces the emotional labor we endure in striving for workplace equality. That's why I continue to stand up for this issue today.

Ultimately, this book is my attempt to articulate these experiences, not just for myself, but for others facing similar struggles. It's not about dwelling on the past but about explaining the dynamics that often lead minorities to feel misunderstood or labeled as difficult. I want this book to be a tool for reflection and action—both for those who face these challenges and for those who may not fully understand them. By sharing my story, I hope to contribute to creating more inclusive environments where all voices are valued equally.

4. Desire to Empower Others and Initiate Change

I wrote this book because I wanted to create a platform where I could fully express my experiences and perspectives—something I often struggle to do verbally, especially in environments where I am the only minority. Despite my efforts to communicate, it often feels as if there's an invisible barrier that prevents my voice from being truly heard and understood. This frustration drove me to find another way to share my story and advocate for change.

The book is not just for immigrants and minorities; it's for allies, leaders, and anyone committed to building more inclusive communities. I wanted to highlight the importance of EDI, share the challenges and triumphs I've encountered, and offer practical steps for creating spaces where everyone can thrive, regardless of their background or identity.

Ultimately, I wrote this book to stand up for all the people I've worked alongside who have been marginalized or treated unfairly. My goal is to normalize the values and perspectives I'm discussing and to break down the barriers that prevent us from treating one another with dignity and respect. Writing felt like the most effective way to reach others, inspire change, and create the deeper understanding that verbal conversations often couldn't achieve.

REFLECTION EXERCISE:

Reflect on your own role in fostering inclusion. Have you ever unknowingly participated in or allowed biases to go unchecked? What steps can you take moving forward to create a more inclusive environment?

_____

_____

_____

_____

_____

CHALLENGE YOURSELF:

As you read on, I encourage you to keep an open mind and ask yourself: What small steps can I take to be an advocate for inclusion, even when it's uncomfortable?

CHAPTER 03
THE HISTORY OF IMMIGRATION IN CANADA

Before diving into current EDI challenges, it's essential to understand the historical context that shaped them. By acknowledging where inequities first emerged, we can better identify their root causes and work toward meaningful solutions.

Canada's approach to immigration has evolved significantly over time, but its history reveals a long-standing preference for European immigrants, creating a legacy that still affects diversity and inclusion efforts today. During the late 19th and early 20th centuries, Canada sought to populate its vast lands primarily with settlers from Britain, France, and other European countries. This Eurocentric strategy—often referred to as the "White Canada" policy—deliberately excluded immigrants from Asia, Africa, and other non-European regions. Policies such as the Chinese Head Tax and the Exclusion Act of 1923 were clear attempts to limit non-European immigration while promoting a predominantly "white" Canadian identity (Canadian Museum of Immigration at Pier 21, n.d.; Government of Canada, 2020).

This approach was not just about numbers—it was rooted in a belief system that sought to maintain Canada's "British character" by enforcing a racial and ethnic hierarchy. The "White Canada" policy prioritized settlers based on their proximity to this ideal, with those of British descent at the top and Asians, Africans, and other racial minorities seen as undesirable. The goal was to preserve what was seen as the cultural superiority of British and European settlers (Venkatesh, 2019; Stasiulis & Bakan, 1997).

These exclusionary policies left a lasting imprint on Canadian institutions, shaping the norms and values around which legal frameworks, social policies, and public services were built. Even after Canada introduced more inclusive policies—such as the points-based immigration system in 1967—the underlying structure of these institutions remained largely unchanged. This continuity means that, while Canada became more diverse, the institutions themselves did not fully adapt to include diverse voices and perspectives (Cambridge University Press & Assessment; The Canadian Encyclopedia).

As a result, new immigrant populations often found themselves navigating systems that were never designed to accommodate their needs. This created barriers in areas such as employment, leadership representation, and access to culturally tailored services. Visible minorities in Canada continue to face disproportionately high unemployment rates and underrepresentation in leadership positions. Between 2006 and 2015, unemployment rates for racialized immigrants in Canada averaged 11.2%—nearly double that of non-racialized Canadians (Canadian Human Rights Commission, 2016; The Canadian Encyclopedia).

Despite Canada's official policy of multiculturalism, introduced in the 1970s, and its reputation as a diverse and welcoming nation, the reality on the ground has been slower to catch up. Multiculturalism often focuses on celebrating cultural diversity without addressing the deeper structural changes needed to support true inclusion. Decision-making structures still reflect the values of a more Eurocentric past, and without fundamental changes, many minority groups continue to face systemic exclusion.

These dynamics directly impact today's conversation around Equity, Diversity, and Inclusion (EDI). The historical preference for European immigrants has left a lasting legacy on Canadian institutions, making it more challenging for newer immigrant communities to achieve equity. Addressing the systemic issues rooted in this history will be essential for creating a genuinely inclusive society.

In the next chapter, we will delve deeper into how these historical biases intersect with unconscious bias and personal insecurities, affecting how people from diverse backgrounds navigate professional and social settings today.

REFLECTION EXERCISE:

Reflect on your workplace or community: Are there any policies, practices, or "norms" that may unintentionally favor certain groups over others? Consider how these norms might have been influenced by historical patterns of inclusion or exclusion, and what steps could be taken to create a more equitable environment.

CHALLENGE YOURSELF:

Identify a Systemic Bias: Look around your organization or community and identify one example of a policy, procedure, or practice that might create barriers for certain groups. Ask yourself: How might this have evolved from historical biases, and who benefits from maintaining the status quo?

CHAPTER 04
UNDERSTANDING UNCONSCIOUS BIAS AND INSECURITY

Unconscious bias is often linked to deep-seated insecurities, but it also stems from a fundamental aspect of human nature. Throughout history, humans have evolved to make snap judgments about others based on cognitive shortcuts. These judgments, which helped early humans survive by quickly assessing potential threats, have persisted into modern times. However, in today's diverse and complex world, these same mental shortcuts can result in unconscious biases—particularly toward people who are different in terms of race, gender, or cultural background (Banaji & Greenwald, 2013).

One of the most pervasive forms of bias is affinity bias—the tendency to favor people who look like us or share similar backgrounds. This instinct to divide people into "us" and "them" categories can lead to the exclusion or unfair treatment of those who are perceived as different. While these biases are often unconscious, they can significantly influence our decisions, behaviors, and interactions (McGee, 2018).

The Intersection of Bias and Insecurity

Unconscious biases are often rooted in social conditioning, but they become particularly pronounced when people feel insecure or threatened. In competitive professional environments, when individuals perceive their competence, authority, or social standing as being challenged—especially by a minority colleague—they may unconsciously resort to behaviors that assert their dominance or undermine the other person. This dynamic is especially evident in workplaces where power and hierarchy play a significant role in shaping relationships.

Research from the *Harvard Business Review* suggests that individuals who feel insecure about their own abilities are more likely to project biases onto others as a way to regain a sense of control (Miller, 2020). In these scenarios, biases become a tool for expressing internal fears and maintaining authority. For minorities, this means navigating not only their workload but also the subtle, competitive behaviors of colleagues who may view them as a threat. Such environments can be particularly challenging because even well-meaning individuals may fall back on biased assumptions when they feel their status is at risk.

When biases are intertwined with insecurity, individuals may unconsciously resist the contributions of minority colleagues, even when those contributions are valid and beneficial. This resistance often manifests in behaviors like interrupting, dismissing ideas, or excluding certain voices from important discussions. Such behaviors create a culture where minority professionals are constantly forced to prove their competence while managing interpersonal tensions. Over time, these microaggressions—small, seemingly insignificant actions or comments that reinforce stereotypes or unequal treatment—accumulate, leading to diminished job satisfaction and mental fatigue (Sue et al., 2007).

Ultimately, understanding the link between bias and insecurity helps us see that these biases are not just surface-level attitudes but are often rooted in deeper fears and self-perceptions. Addressing this intersection is crucial because it shifts the focus from simply identifying biases to understanding the emotional drivers behind them. By tackling these underlying insecurities, individuals and organizations can create a more inclusive environment where people feel empowered to contribute their best ideas without fear of dismissal or exclusion.

Personal Experience Example: The Subtle Competitiveness of Colleagues

Throughout my career, I've encountered subtle, competitive behaviors from colleagues who seemed to place themselves above me, even before fully getting to know me. This dynamic often became more apparent when colleagues realized I held a comparable or higher-level position. It sometimes felt as though my role and authority were diminished—not based on my capabilities, but due to preconceived perceptions. In several workplaces there were noticeable patterns of preferential treatment for those who shared more similarities—whether in language, culture, or background—with the majority group. While some colleagues integrated easily into the team, others, particularly those from minority backgrounds, faced more challenges in building rapport and being fully accepted. This pattern was subtle but evident in various aspects of our professional interactions.

One incident that stands out occurred during a training session I was leading for a group of colleagues. Although I was tasked with providing valuable information and updates, some participants displayed subtle resistance to my guidance, offering short, dismissive responses and occasionally avoiding direct engagement. This response suggested that my role and credibility were being questioned, not based on the content I presented but likely due to an unconscious bias about who should be leading. Research shows that women and minorities in leadership positions often face additional scrutiny and skepticism about their authority, even when their credentials are comparable to their peers (Catalyst, 2020).

Another situation arose when a supervisor was absent, and my colleague and I were given an opportunity to implement changes to processes we had previously discussed. After receiving support from our director, I brought these ideas to my colleague for input, but my suggestions were dismissed outright. Initially, I assumed my colleague might have felt left out of earlier conversations, so I made a point of including them in all subsequent discussions. However, a pattern emerged: while they would privately acknowledge and support my ideas, in larger meetings, they would often shift the focus to their own preferences, effectively sidelining my contributions. This behavior aligned with research showing that unconscious biases can lead people to undermine the contributions of colleagues they perceive as "different," particularly in collaborative environments (McKinsey & Company, 2021).

This tension was challenging because it appeared to stem not from the ideas themselves but from a reluctance to share credit or collaborate on equal footing. When I was tasked to update them on new processes, which I frequently did as part of my role, they often seemed disengaged. It was clear that they weren't paying attention or interested in the conversation. Their responses were brief, and they didn't seem to be listening, making it feel as though my input was not valued or important. Despite my efforts to present information in a neutral, respectful tone, these interactions consistently felt strained and dismissive.

One conversation revealed another layer of unconscious bias regarding language. My colleague suggested that individuals with strong accents might struggle to communicate effectively and that others would feel more comfortable speaking with someone who had a "familiar" way of speaking. This observation implied that fluency in English—specifically, the way it was spoken—was being used as a proxy for competence, reinforcing a subtle hierarchy in communication. As research shows, non-native English speakers are often viewed as less capable, not because of their skills but because of the perception that an accent impacts their effectiveness (Lev-Ari & Keysar, 2010).

As someone who speaks English as a second language, I found this particularly concerning. These kinds of remarks, while often dismissed as "practical" concerns, contribute to the marginalization of non-native speakers, implying that their contributions are less valuable. Studies highlight that biases around accents can lead to significant disadvantages in professional settings, as individuals are judged not by their competence but by how closely they conform to linguistic norms (Lippi-Green, 2012). This mindset creates unnecessary barriers for non-native speakers, suggesting that their ideas and input are less worthy of consideration.

When I attempted to discuss the impact of these comments, the colleague framed their remarks as purely pragmatic, explaining that they didn't intend to offend. However, the reluctance to engage in a deeper conversation about the implications of such views left me feeling isolated. This kind of deflection is common when unconscious biases are raised; instead of reflecting on the underlying issue, individuals often focus on avoiding discomfort. Research supports this, indicating that people in majority groups frequently avoid conversations about race, language, and bias because they find these topics uncomfortable (Sue et al., 2007).

At times, when I raised broader concerns about collaboration or process improvements, the colleague would start to tear up or visibly get upset, often walking out of the conversation before we could resolve anything. This behavior made it difficult to foster meaningful dialogue, as emotional reactions frequently shut down the opportunity for productive discussions. While these responses may have been rooted in personal discomfort, they prevented us from addressing important issues, leaving the problems unresolved.

These responses are frustrating because minorities are often forced to confront uncomfortable realities—without the option to walk away. Meanwhile, those in the majority have the privilege of avoiding these conversations. It became clear that when the majority shields themselves from discomfort, they reinforce a system that prioritizes their emotional safety over the growth and well-being of others. By opting out of these necessary but difficult conversations, they miss crucial opportunities for personal development and perpetuate systemic inequalities.

Studies show that minorities in predominantly white or majority environments experience heightened "racial isolation" and must often develop strategies to cope with dismissive or hostile behaviors, all while managing cultural stereotypes (Psychology Today, 2018). This emotional labor is taxing and leads to higher rates of burnout and mental health challenges. Minorities are frequently expected to demonstrate resilience in environments that don't always provide the support necessary for their success (Harris et al., 2018).

Over time, my efforts to address these dynamics were sometimes met with perceptions that I was being "difficult" or "overly sensitive." This response is common when individuals raise concerns about unconscious biases—defensiveness often replaces reflection, making it challenging to foster genuine inclusivity (Sue et al., 2007). My experience is not unique; many minorities face similar challenges when they attempt to address deep-rooted issues in professional environments.

Eventually, after numerous attempts to engage in dialogue and advocate for change, I recognized that addressing these concerns in this particular environment would be an uphill battle. My efforts were seen as "challenging the norm" rather than contributing to a more inclusive workplace culture. While I eventually moved on from that environment, I hope that some of the conversations I initiated sparked reflection within the organization.

This experience highlights the emotional labor minorities invest in trying to create spaces where their contributions are valued equally. For true inclusion to take place, there must be an understanding that these efforts are not a burden but an essential aspect of creating a workplace where all voices can thrive. Collaboration and inclusivity cannot exist without confronting uncomfortable truths and engaging in the necessary, albeit difficult, conversations that lead to growth.

Research Insight: The Competitive Dynamics of Bias

Research supports this observation, showing that minority employees, particularly Asian professionals, are often viewed as "doers" rather than leaders, reinforcing subtle hierarchies in the workplace (McKinsey, 2021). Additionally, studies such as Harvard's Implicit Association Test (IAT) demonstrate that people unconsciously associate positive traits more easily with those who share their racial or cultural backgrounds (Harvard Gazette, 2021). This bias may manifest as competition when individuals from the majority group feel threatened by the abilities or achievements of minority colleagues, whom they may subconsciously view as less capable until proven otherwise.

Unconscious Bias vs. Microaggressions: Understanding the Difference

While unconscious bias refers to the underlying attitudes or stereotypes people hold, microaggressions are the outward expressions of these biases—manifesting in subtle but harmful actions and words. Microaggressions are not always intentional; they can be as simple as asking someone, "Where are you really from?" or making backhanded compliments like, "You're very articulate for someone from your background." Even when meant as praise, these comments reinforce stereotypes and contribute to a culture of exclusion.

In addition to the unconscious biases I experienced, I also encountered microaggressions from my colleague and others, which served as clear indicators that the challenges I faced weren't solely rooted in competitiveness or personality differences—they were directly related to Equity, Diversity, and Inclusion (EDI) issues. For example, comments about language fluency or assumptions about my background weren't just offhand remarks; they reflected deeper stereotypes and reinforced my position as an "outsider." These microaggressions, though often subtle, were strong reminders of the barriers I was up against, making it clear that this was not just a professional rivalry but a reflection of broader systemic issues.

For many, it's easy to question whether experiences like mine truly fall under the realm of EDI. However, the numerous microaggressions and unconscious biases I observed over time strongly validate that these were not isolated incidents but part of a larger pattern of exclusion. These experiences, combined with the constant need to prove myself in environments where my contributions were undervalued, point to the very real EDI challenges that minorities face in professional settings.

Concrete Examples of Microaggressions in Professional Settings

Microaggressions often manifest in subtle yet harmful ways that can be difficult to recognize. Here are some common examples that illustrate how these behaviors undermine inclusivity:

- **Interrupting or Overlooking Contributions in Meetings:** When minority voices are regularly interrupted or spoken over, it signals that their perspectives are less valuable.
- **Backhanded Compliments:** Comments like "You speak English so well for a foreigner" may be intended as praise but imply surprise at their competence.
- **Questioning Authority Based on Identity:** Asking for confirmation from a senior employee when a minority professional has already provided the answer diminishes their expertise.
- **Excessive Focus on Accents or Physical Appearance:** Commenting on accents or how "exotic" someone looks, even if meant as a compliment, can make individuals feel like outsiders.

The Impact of Microaggressions on Team Dynamics

When microaggressions are allowed to persist, they don't just harm the individual—they also undermine team cohesion and reduce psychological safety, leading to lower morale and less effective collaboration across the entire group. Over time, this can create a toxic work environment where innovation and productivity suffer, as people become more focused on navigating interpersonal tensions than on contributing their best ideas.

Even if these comments or actions are unintentional, their cumulative effect can create a work environment where minorities feel unseen and unwelcome, leading to a decline in overall team morale and engagement.

Addressing Unconscious Bias and Mitigating Insecurity: Moving from Intent to Impact

One of the key challenges in addressing unconscious bias is shifting the focus from intent to impact. When biases are intertwined with insecurity or competitiveness, individuals may rationalize their behavior as harmless or even justified. However, organizations must establish a clear standard that looks at the *impact* on the person experiencing these behaviors, not just the intent of the speaker.

Creating an environment where individuals feel supported and valued for their unique strengths—rather than competing to "fit in"—can help reduce the insecurities that often drive biased behaviors. This involves acknowledging and addressing not just overt biases but also the underlying fears or competitive dynamics that fuel them.

Organizational Responsibility: Building a Culture of Accountability

Organizations must create a safe space for employees to voice concerns and establish a process for addressing them promptly and consistently. Leaders play a crucial role in setting the tone for what is acceptable in the workplace. By implementing clear policies and holding people accountable—regardless of intent—organizations can build a culture where biases and insecurities do not translate into exclusionary behaviors.

- **Create Clear Guidelines on Behavior:** Establish clear expectations around language and conduct, and ensure that employees understand what constitutes a microaggression or bias.

- **Provide Continuous Training:** Offer ongoing education on recognizing and addressing unconscious bias, ensuring that the focus is not just on "awareness" but on creating actionable change.
- **Support Those Who Speak Up:** Encourage open dialogue, provide support for employees who raise concerns, and ensure that feedback is taken seriously without fear of retaliation.

Culture-change Example: Starbucks' Anti-Bias Training

In response to a racial bias incident in 2018, Starbucks closed more than 8,000 stores across the U.S. for a day to provide company-wide anti-bias training. This initiative aimed to address the unconscious biases employees might carry and ensure that everyone felt welcome in their stores, regardless of race, background, or language. While it was a bold move, the training highlighted how widespread unconscious bias can be and how essential it is for organizations to address it proactively. The initiative demonstrated that shifting from awareness to action requires a comprehensive, organization-wide commitment (Wharton School, 2018).

Final Reflections: Moving from Awareness to Action

Ultimately, addressing unconscious biases and their link to insecurity is not just a step toward inclusivity—it's about fostering environments where everyone feels empowered to bring their best selves to work, free from judgment or prejudice. Only by creating spaces where subtle forms of exclusion are identified and addressed can we move toward genuine inclusion.

REFLECTION EXERCISE: EXPLORING YOUR OWN BIASES AND INSECURITIES

1. **Identify a Personal Bias:** Think about a time when you made an assumption about someone based on superficial traits, such as their appearance, accent, or cultural background. What were you feeling in that moment? Was there any insecurity or fear underlying your reaction? Take a few minutes to reflect and write down what may have triggered that response.

   _____
   _____
   _____

2. **Consider Your Professional Environment:** Reflect on your workplace or community. Can you recall a situation where you might have unconsciously favored someone who was similar to you (e.g., similar background, interests, or work style)? What led you to make that decision, and what impact did it have on those who were excluded?

   _____
   _____
   _____

3. **Examine Your Response to Feedback:** Have you ever felt defensive or threatened when receiving feedback, especially from someone you considered to be an "outsider"? Think about how your own insecurities may have played a role in how you responded. What steps can you take to approach similar situations with a more open mind in the future?

_____

_____

_____

CHALLENGE YOURSELF: SHIFTING FROM AWARENESS TO ACTION

1. **Actively Seek Out Different Perspectives:** Challenge yourself to reach out to colleagues or acquaintances who have different backgrounds or viewpoints. Listen to their experiences and insights, especially when it comes to issues you may not have considered. Make it a point to regularly engage with diverse perspectives and resist the urge to default to familiar viewpoints.

2. **Catch and Correct Microaggressions:** Pay attention to the subtle ways unconscious bias might show up in your behavior—such as interrupting, making assumptions, or giving backhanded compliments. When you catch yourself doing this, stop and rephrase your words, and then consider why you reacted that way. Commit to correcting these behaviors in real-time.

3. **Create a Personal Accountability Plan:** Identify one bias or insecurity you struggle with and create a simple plan to address it. For example, if you tend to feel competitive or threatened by minority colleagues, challenge yourself to support and amplify their contributions in meetings or projects. Set specific actions, like giving positive feedback or inviting them to share their ideas in group settings.

CHAPTER 05 SEEING THE WORLD AS A MINORITY

Equity, Diversity, and Inclusion (EDI) require more than just awareness of inequality—they demand deep reflection on how different people experience the world. Being a minority isn't just about race or ethnicity; it's about being the outsider in any setting. Whether you're a woman in a male-dominated workplace, a non-native English speaker in a fast-paced meeting, or simply the only person of your background in a room full of people who share common experiences, the challenges are numerous: your voice might not be heard, your contributions may be overlooked, and you might feel isolated.

Growing up, I often felt this way. My experiences of being the only Asian in a predominantly white environment in North America gave me early insights into how unconscious biases shape our interactions. This chapter delves into the nuances of seeing the world through a minority lens, exploring the obstacles minorities face and the strategies they adopt to overcome them.

Navigating Leadership as a Minority: The Challenges of Leading with a Collaborative Approach

When I took on a leadership role at my daughter's sports club, I wasn't driven by a desire for power or control. Instead, I saw it as an opportunity for personal growth—a chance to challenge myself and learn what it truly means to lead in a complex environment. I wanted to establish a space where every member felt valued, respected, and empowered to contribute. To me, creating a positive and inclusive atmosphere seemed like an obvious goal—one that should resonate with everyone. But this vision was met with more resistance than I had ever anticipated.

As I began my presidency, I realized that being a minority leader came with an additional layer of complexity. When

I first joined the club, I saw how a small group of individuals dominated discussions and made decisions that served their own interests. They would often disregard other members' opinions, creating a toxic atmosphere where dissenting voices were either silenced or dismissed. When these behaviors went unchallenged, it drove out valuable members who felt unheard and marginalized. I believed that if I stepped into a leadership role, I could address these power imbalances and create a more collaborative environment.

From the start, I emphasized a new approach to decision-making. I promoted group discussions where every voice was heard and stressed the importance of respecting each other's contributions, no matter how different. I was upfront about my belief that leadership should be about serving the group rather than exerting control. I openly shared my vision: "If you're here to push your own agenda, this is not the place for you. Our focus should be on what's best for the club and the children, not on any one person's benefit."

At first, this strategy seemed to work. I saw members who had previously been hesitant start to speak up. We began using a democratic voting system where everyone had an equal say, and I felt like we were finally building a space where collaboration and mutual respect guided our decisions. However, as we made progress, those who had been used to dominating the meetings started to push back. They arrived at meetings armed with counterarguments, aiming not to contribute to the discussion but to disrupt and undermine any decision that didn't align with their personal interests.

The situation escalated quickly. They began using aggressive tones, interrupting others, and even resorting to personal attacks. Despite my efforts to remain calm and reinforce our commitment to collective decision-making, they went out of their way to discredit me, pointing out trivial mistakes and spreading misinformation. The hostility reached a peak at a public meeting when facts were twisted and false accusations were made, and many members believed them simply because they were louder and more assertive.

This dynamic reflected a common experience for minority leaders in predominantly Western spaces. Research shows that Asian leaders who promote harmony and consensus-driven decision-making are often seen as weak or lacking authority in cultures that prioritize assertiveness and individual achievement (Ferdman & Sagiv, 2012; Gundling, 2016). This can lead to a perception that they are unfit to lead, even when their approach is more inclusive and collaborative. In my case, my efforts to create a safe space for diverse perspectives were interpreted as an inability to control the room.

But it wasn't just the resistance that made this experience so draining—it was the emotional labor of having to navigate these interactions day after day. As a minority leader, I was expected to remain composed and respectful even when faced with hostility, while my opponents could openly display aggression without consequence. Research indicates that minorities often experience heightened levels of stress and emotional fatigue because they must constantly adapt to environments that challenge their legitimacy and identity as leaders (Harris et al., 2018). This double standard—where I was held to a higher standard of behavior while others acted out without repercussion—felt not only unfair but unsustainable.

The burden was particularly heavy because, as a minority, I did not have the option to retreat into avoidance. While some of my colleagues could say, "I don't do well with conflicts" or "I'm not comfortable in these situations," I did not have the luxury of stepping back. I had to address these conflicts head-on, not just to defend myself but to preserve the inclusive environment I was striving to build. Research supports this experience: minorities, especially those in leadership roles, are frequently expected to confront difficult conversations and navigate conflicts to prove their credibility (Sue et al., 2007). This added layer of expectation creates a cycle of heightened stress and emotional labor, often leading to burnout and disillusionment (Harris et al., 2018).

Over time, the atmosphere in our meetings became more toxic. Even minor disagreements would be met with eye-rolling, loud sighs, and dismissive gestures, making others reluctant to speak up. The few times I tried to address these behaviors privately, I was met with denial and defensiveness. Their consistent response was to deny any wrongdoing and deflect by questioning my judgment. Each attempt I made to resolve these issues was turned against me, making it feel like I was walking a tightrope—one misstep, and I would be labeled as the "problem" rather than the solution.

Eventually, I realized that I could not change the behavior of people who saw empathy and respect as weaknesses. It became apparent that my approach—based on harmony, mutual respect, and collective decision-making—could not succeed in a space dominated by those who valued power and control above all else. Research shows that without a collective willingness to engage in self-reflection and address these power imbalances, inclusive leadership styles are unlikely to succeed in environments that prioritize individual dominance (Miller, 2020).

The decision to leave was heartbreaking, but it was necessary. I felt as though I had failed, not just in my role but in my vision for what the club could have become. The experience taught me that until people are willing to confront their own biases, respect others' viewpoints, and value diverse leadership styles, creating truly inclusive spaces will remain a difficult and arduous journey. The challenge for minority leaders is not just to lead effectively but to do so in environments that are inherently resistant to the values they bring.

Reflecting on this experience, I see now that achieving true inclusivity requires more than a willingness to listen—it demands a willingness to confront uncomfortable truths and rethink what leadership looks like. For Asian leaders like myself, the emphasis on respect, empathy, and team orientation must be balanced against the Western preference for assertiveness and control. Unless everyone practices mutual respect, cultivates empathy, and becomes more aware of their unconscious biases and urge to dominate, it will be nearly impossible to foster a harmonious team environment in North American contexts.

Creating inclusive leadership is not just about changing systems—it's about changing mindsets. And that, I believe, will take years of persistent effort, education, and self-reflection from everyone involved.

The Professional Reality: Speaking Up in Group Meetings

One of the most challenging spaces for minorities is the group meeting—especially when it's fast-paced. My experience in North American workplaces was a stark contrast to the environment I had grown up in, where allowing others to finish speaking was a deeply ingrained practice. In group meetings in North America, I often found myself waiting for the perfect moment to share my thoughts, only to realize that by the time I was ready to contribute, the conversation had shifted, or the meeting was already over.

This reflects a common experience for many minorities, which my EDI committee colleagues and I often described as being both visible and invisible at the same time. As minorities, we are often highly visible, with any misstep being scrutinized, while at the same time our contributions and voices can go unnoticed or ignored. For instance, minorities frequently feel that they must work harder to avoid mistakes, as our errors are amplified, whereas the same mistakes made by Caucasian colleagues might be overlooked. This sense of constant visibility for the wrong reasons—coupled with invisibility when we try to share ideas—creates a dynamic where we feel we cannot afford to make any mistakes. This is another example of the "prove it again" bias mentioned in Chapter 2.

Navigating this kind of unforgiving environment led to significant frustration and meant that I was always on high alert. Over the years, I had to learn to be more assertive, which felt unnatural to me. My cultural background emphasized thoughtful pauses and reflection, while the meetings I attended valued quick exchanges. I soon realized that my challenge wasn't unique—many minorities, especially those who speak English as a second language, face similar hurdles. Research has shown that non-native speakers often process information differently, sometimes taking longer to formulate their thoughts and responses (The Independent, 2019; Workplace Communication, 2020). This can result in their contributions being overlooked—not because they have less to offer, but because the structure of the meeting doesn't accommodate their communication style.

Connection to Unconscious Bias: Why Some Voices Go Unheard

This issue is tied directly to unconscious bias, as discussed in Chapter 4. Unconscious biases often lead people to favor voices and opinions that feel familiar—those that align with the majority perspective. In meetings, this bias can manifest as individuals unintentionally dismissing or interrupting those who speak more slowly or differently. This bias, often stemming from insecurities or the desire to maintain control of the conversation (Harvard Gazette, 2021), can significantly hinder inclusive collaboration.

For example, when facilitators unconsciously prioritize fast-paced conversations, they may overlook the fact that minorities—particularly those who speak English as a second language—need a little more time to process and share their thoughts. The result is that these voices, which often bring unique perspectives, go unheard. This is a missed opportunity for innovation and better decision-making. Studies show that teams with diverse perspectives consistently perform better (CIPD, 2020).

Individualism vs. Collectivism: A Broader Cultural Disconnect

The experience in Alabama highlighted another fundamental challenge: the stark contrast between individualistic and collectivist values. While Western cultures often champion individualism and assertiveness, these concepts can create barriers for those of us from more collectivist backgrounds. Individualism encourages self-expression and assertiveness, but it often fails to accommodate the voices of those who were raised to prioritize collective well-being and group harmony.

In settings where individuality is celebrated, I found that my more reflective and consensus-driven communication style was frequently misinterpreted as passivity or lack of engagement. This was not due to malice but rather a blend of unconscious biases and differing cultural norms. In professional environments, this disconnect became more pronounced. The emphasis on quick decision-making and assertiveness in meetings often made it difficult for my perspectives to be heard.

This is a common struggle for many minorities: navigating a world that encourages personal freedom but doesn't always create space for everyone to express themselves equally. Individualism, while empowering in some ways, can overlook the value of collective harmony and result in environments that prioritize the loudest voices over the most thoughtful contributions.

This realization ties back to professional settings, where prioritizing assertiveness over reflection can silence those whose voices are crucial for building diverse, collaborative environments. Inclusivity requires more than just encouraging self-expression—it demands creating room for diverse perspectives and ensuring that everyone feels valued, regardless of their communication style or cultural background.

The Consequences of Being Unheard

Being consistently overlooked or excluded can lead to a profound sense of isolation. Many minorities in the workplace feel like outsiders, even when they're part of a team. Research shows that minorities are significantly more likely to leave a workplace where they feel unrepresented. For instance, a study in the UK revealed that 42% of Black employees had resigned due to a lack of workplace diversity and inclusion, compared to just 26% of white employees (The Independent, 2019; Community Solutions, 2019).

This lack of representation and feeling unheard can lead to job dissatisfaction, burnout, and ultimately, higher turnover rates. Speaking up requires emotional energy and resilience—especially when you're unsure whether your concerns will be taken seriously. Without supportive mechanisms in place, leaving often seems like the only solution.

Creating More Inclusive Meetings

The key to preventing this outcome is creating spaces where everyone's voice is valued. Leaders and facilitators must be mindful of group dynamics, particularly when minority voices are present. Simple strategies like pausing to invite input from those who haven't spoken or allowing extra time for reflection can make a significant difference. Research suggests that diverse teams perform better when all members have an opportunity to contribute their perspectives (CIPD, 2020).

Navigating the Complexities of Inclusion

The experiences shared in this chapter illustrate the complexities of navigating a world that doesn't always value diverse voices. From being overlooked in meetings to managing cultural differences in communication styles, minorities often face an uphill battle to be truly heard and understood. Yet, these challenges are not insurmountable. Understanding the impact of these dynamics is the first step toward building spaces where everyone's voice can be appreciated and included.

Moving forward, it's crucial to reflect on the historical and systemic roots of these disparities. In the next chapter, we will explore the practice of Indigenous land acknowledgements, examining their significance as a tool for genuine reflection and a step toward reconciling with the past. By embracing these acknowledgements meaningfully, we can better understand the broader context of inclusion and respect in the communities we are part of.

REFLECTION EXERCISES: SEEING THE WORLD AS A MINORITY

1. **Observe Group Dynamics in a Recent Setting:** Recall a recent meeting or social gathering. Who were the most vocal participants? Who spoke the least? Why do you think that is? Reflect on what factors—such as language barriers, cultural norms, or unconscious biases—might have influenced who felt comfortable contributing and who didn't.

   _____
   _____
   _____

2. **Reflect on a Time You Felt Like an Outsider:** Think about a time when you were the only person in a group who didn't share the same background, interests, or experiences as the majority. How did that make you feel? What thoughts or emotions did you experience? Did the group make an effort to include you? If not, what could they have done differently?

   _____
   _____
   _____

3. **Think About Cultural Communication Styles:** Consider your own communication style. Do you tend to speak quickly, wait your turn, or prefer silence to reflect? Now think about people you've worked with from different cultural backgrounds. How might their communication style differ from yours? How can you adapt your own style to create space for others?

_____

_____

_____

4. **Consider the Emotional Labor of Minorities:** Reflect on how it might feel to constantly navigate a space where your voice isn't easily heard. What impact do you think this would have on a person's motivation, mental health, and job satisfaction? How can you contribute to creating a culture that values these voices?

_____

_____

_____

CHALLENGE YOURSELF: AMPLIFYING MINORITY VOICES IN PROFESSIONAL SETTINGS

1. **Be an Active Ally in Meetings:** Next time you're in a meeting, make it a point to observe the dynamics. If you notice that certain voices are being interrupted, overlooked, or not participating, intentionally create space for those individuals to share. For example, you could say, "I'd like to hear from [Name], as I don't think we've had a chance to hear their perspective yet."

2. **Examine Your Own Communication Style:** Reflect on whether your communication style might unintentionally exclude others. Do you tend to dominate conversations or value speed over thoughtful contributions? Challenge yourself to slow down, ask more questions, and be mindful of how your approach could impact colleagues who may have a different communication style.

3. **Advocate for Structural Changes:** Advocate for structural changes in meeting formats that encourage more inclusive participation. Suggest implementing practices like "round-robin" style input, assigning a moderator to manage the flow of conversation, or setting a policy where everyone has equal opportunity to speak before closing a discussion.

4. **Amplify Underrepresented Voices:** When someone from a minority group shares an idea, actively reinforce it by acknowledging their contribution. For example, say, "I think [Name] made a great point earlier about X. Could we explore that idea further?" This helps ensure that diverse perspectives aren't lost in the shuffle.

5. **Create Space for Reflection:** If you lead meetings or discussions, introduce short pauses for participants to gather their thoughts before moving on to the next topic. This allows those who may need more time to process to feel more comfortable sharing, and it fosters a more inclusive environment where every participant has time to contribute meaningfully.

CHAPTER 06

INDIGENOUS LAND ACKNOWLEDGEMENT: A STEP TOWARD GENUINE REFLECTION

In recent years, land acknowledgements have become a common practice across Canada, particularly in large organizations, to recognize Indigenous territories. However, I've noticed that for many, these acknowledgements seem more like a formal courtesy—something to check off the list—rather than a deeply reflective practice. I want to challenge this approach and encourage people to take the core meaning of land acknowledgements seriously.

When we acknowledge the Indigenous peoples who have welcomed us to their land, it should serve as an opportunity to reflect on how we are treating those around us. Can we extend that acknowledgement to the everyday relationships we have with our colleagues, neighbors, and community members? Why can't we thank each other for sharing the space and land we stand on, ensuring we treat each other with respect and equality?

At its heart, a land acknowledgement challenges us to examine how we treat one another and whether we are fostering respect, care, and inclusivity. Based on my experience, I believe that when we truly remove our biases and treat everyone fairly and equally, we can begin to experience genuine equality and harmony. This belief is something I was taught as a child in Japan, where respect for others and coexistence is a core value.

However, when I moved to North America, I initially struggled to understand why people seemed more focused on individualism rather than collective well-being. After over 20 years of living in Canada, I am finally hearing discussions around acceptance and coexistence. This gives me hope because I believe this is the first step toward building real harmony in society.

This isn't just my personal belief; research and conversations within Canadian institutions support the idea that land acknowledgements should be tied to meaningful action. For example, institutions like Dalhousie and McGill universities emphasize that land acknowledgements must go beyond words—they must involve reflection and inspire action toward equity and inclusion (McGill University, 2020). Acknowledging the land without addressing the injustices faced by Indigenous communities becomes an empty gesture (Amnesty International Canada, 2020).

Furthermore, efforts must continue in the context of the ongoing reconciliation process. Organizations such as Amnesty International have noted that land acknowledgements serve as small acts of resistance against the erasure of Indigenous rights, yet they must be paired with a commitment to protecting these rights and ensuring justice for Indigenous peoples (The Peak, 2021).

PRACTICAL EXERCISE:

Research the Indigenous history of the land where you live. Consider attending local Indigenous events, supporting Indigenous-led initiatives, or advocating for the rights of Indigenous communities. Reflect on how your everyday actions can contribute to a more inclusive society and how you can honor the land acknowledgement with meaningful steps.

CHAPTER 07
EMPOWERING CHANGE: TAKING THE FIRST STEP

Despite various EDI (Equity, Diversity, and Inclusion) initiatives, many individuals and organizations continue to face significant challenges in fostering true inclusivity. As discussed in earlier chapters, these obstacles often stem from outdated organizational structures, deeply ingrained unconscious biases, and a lack of intentional strategies to address inequality. Another critical issue is that many organizations do not perceive EDI as a pressing priority unless compelled by external forces, such as regulatory mandates or societal pressure. For example, gender equality in workplaces made significant strides only after legal frameworks, such as quotas and pay equity laws, required action from organizations. Without similar pressure or accountability measures for EDI, organizations may relegate these efforts to secondary priorities, limiting their impact (McKinsey & Company, 2020).

Understanding these barriers is the first step toward building more equitable environments. This chapter summarizes the key EDI challenges faced by both individuals and organizations and provides actionable steps to address and hopefully overcome these barriers. With these insights, I hope to empower readers to advocate for change, whether as leaders within organizations or as individuals striving to create more inclusive spaces.

Organizational Challenges and Solutions

1. STRUCTURAL AND SYSTEM BARRIERS

Problem: One of the fundamental challenges with EDI initiatives is that many organizations do not treat it as a priority. Without external pressure, such as governmental mandates or societal accountability, organizations often focus on short-term business objectives rather than making systemic changes. This lack of urgency perpetuates inequities in hiring, promotion, and representation in leadership roles. Historically, progress in areas like gender equality has often only come after the introduction of legal frameworks—such as quotas and mandated reporting—that enforced changes. Without similar accountability measures for EDI, organizations may continue to deprioritize inclusivity.

In addition to this lack of urgency, organizational structures themselves often favor the majority in decision-making processes. This results in inequities in hiring, promotion, and representation in leadership roles. As a result, minority employees face significant barriers to advancement, and diverse voices are not fully represented at higher levels. This lack of minority representation in decision-making positions is particularly harmful because when all decision-makers come from the majority, it becomes difficult for them to validate or understand the experiences of minorities. When minorities feel they are being mistreated for unjust reasons, it is challenging for the majority to fully grasp or empathize with what minorities are going through. This perpetuates an environment of exclusion and makes it harder to address issues of inequality, leading to limited opportunities for innovation and inclusive progress.

SOLUTION:

   a. **Increased Governmental Oversight:** To ensure that EDI becomes a core organizational priority, similar accountability measures as those seen in gender equality mandates should be considered. Government agencies and industry leaders could establish clear EDI reporting requirements and penalties for non-compliance. This will create the necessary urgency for organizations to address inequities.
   b. **Analyze Employment and Diversity Data:** Start by analyzing internal employment data, including the ratio of majority to minority employees, gender representation, and leadership demographics. By breaking this data down by department, organizations can identify where diversity is lacking and develop targeted strategies.

c. **Revamp Hiring and Promotion Processes:** Implement structured, transparent hiring and promotion practices that prioritize diverse candidates and ensure representation across all levels. Use data-driven methods such as blind recruitment and standardized evaluation criteria to minimize biases.
d. **Set Diversity and Inclusion Goals:** Establish specific, measurable diversity targets and track progress regularly. Leadership should commit to achieving these goals and adjust strategies as needed to ensure representation and equity.
e. **Create Systems for Inclusive Meetings:** Leaders and facilitators should develop systems within meetings that ensure everyone's input is heard. This could involve using structured methods, like round-robin or moderated discussions, to prevent dominant voices from overshadowing others. In addition, facilitators should ensure that the dynamics of the meeting attendees are taken into account beforehand, recognizing that diverse voices might be missing. If it's determined that a particular group is underrepresented, this should be acknowledged at the start of the meeting, and efforts should be made to bring those missing voices into future discussions whenever possible. This acknowledgement helps to highlight gaps in representation and can drive more conscious inclusion efforts across teams.

2. MAJORITY FOCUSED ENVIRONMENTS AND INTERNAL PROCESSES

Problem: Minorities, particularly minority leaders, face additional stress navigating competitive workplaces where assertiveness and dominance are prized traits. This creates a "prove yourself" mentality that can be exhausting and demoralizing, especially when collaborative or consensus-based approaches are seen as signs of weakness.

SOLUTION:

a. **Redefine Leadership Norms:** Provide EDI training for leaders on inclusive leadership styles and encourage diverse approaches that prioritize collaboration, respect, and shared decision-making.
b. **Address Bias in Team Dynamics:** Establish norms for respectful communication and ensure that meetings are structured to allow for balanced contributions. Use strategies like round-robin input and moderated discussions to prevent dominant voices from taking over.
c. **Amplify Underrepresented Voices:** Actively create space for minority voices, recognizing that communication styles vary and that assertiveness should not be the sole measure of leadership potential.

3. FAILURE TO ADDRESS HARMFUL BEHAVIORS

Problem: Organizations often fail to hold individuals accountable for harmful behaviors, such as microaggressions and biased comments, which perpetuate a culture that tolerates exclusion. Minorities who challenge these behaviors are frequently labeled as difficult or not a "cultural fit."

SOLUTION:

a. **Enforce Accountability Measures:** Implement clear policies outlining what constitutes exclusionary conduct and establish specific consequences for such behaviors. Regularly train all employees on these guidelines and encourage leadership to model inclusive behaviors.
b. **Encourage Inclusive Leadership:** Train leaders on how to recognize, address, and prevent harmful behaviors. Leaders should be held accountable for maintaining an inclusive environment and should be evaluated on their ability to manage diverse teams effectively.
c. **Ongoing EDI Education and Integration:** Provide continuous EDI education through seminars, workshops, and ongoing discussions. This ensures that all employees, espe-

cially those in leadership, are consistently thinking about how they can contribute to a more inclusive workplace.

4. GROUPTHINK AND HOMOGENEITY

Problem: Homogeneous teams are prone to groupthink, stifling diverse viewpoints and reducing innovation. This results in decisions that fail to consider a broad range of perspectives, ultimately limiting organizational success.

SOLUTION:

   a. **Diversify Team Composition:** Create mixed teams that include individuals from various backgrounds to enhance decision-making. Use structured frameworks for discussions to ensure that all voices are heard and considered before finalizing decisions.
   b. **Introduce Anonymous Feedback Options:** Implement systems that allow employees to anonymously share dissenting opinions and provide suggestions, ensuring that minority viewpoints are included in organizational decisions.

5. THE EMOTIONAL TOLL ON MINORITIES AND LACK OF SUPPORT SYSTEMS

Problem: Exclusion and repeated microaggressions lead to burnout, isolation, and high turnover among minority employees, causing a revolving door effect. Further, minority employees often lack safe spaces to share concerns and are underrepresented in leadership positions, making it challenging to navigate workplaces built around majority norms. This lack of support can lead to feelings of isolation and disengagement, resulting in lost talent and a negative impact on the organization's diversity efforts.

SOLUTION:

   a. **Offer Mental Health and Support Resources:** Provide culturally sensitive mental health resources and create peer support networks for minority employees to share their experiences.

b. **Recognize and Reward EDI Efforts:** Actively acknowledge and reward contributions to EDI initiatives, ensuring that EDI work is valued and not seen as an "extra" burden on minority employees.
c. **Create Employee Resource Groups (ERGs) and Mentorship Programs:** Establish formal ERGs and mentorship initiatives that connect minority employees with allies and mentors. These programs should be actively supported and resourced by the organization to foster community and development.

Individual Challenges and Solutions

1. LACK OF UNDERSTANDING AND SUPPORT FOR MINORITIES

Problem: Many minorities experience feelings of isolation or exclusion in environments where their perspectives and needs are not fully understood. This lack of support, combined with microaggressions and biases, can erode confidence and mental well-being, making it harder for minority individuals to thrive.

SOLUTION:

a. **Foster Empathy and Understanding:** As a society, we must take active steps to better understand the unique experiences of minorities. This involves listening without judgment and creating spaces where minorities feel comfortable sharing their stories. Acknowledge their experiences and work to understand the challenges they face, rather than dismissing or minimizing them.
b. **Offer Meaningful Support:** Beyond passive listening, be proactive in offering support. This could include mentorship programs, peer support groups, or simply being a consistent ally. By validating the struggles that minorities face and helping them navigate challenges, we can contribute to more inclusive and supportive environments.

2. LACK OF AWARENESS OF UNCONSCIOUS BIAS AND INSECURITY

Problem: As a society, we are all susceptible to unconscious biases, such as affinity bias, which leads us to favor those who resemble us in background or behavior. These subtle biases often manifest in exclusionary behaviors that hinder inclusivity and make it difficult for diverse perspectives to be heard and valued. Additionally, personal insecurities—such as fear of being challenged or discomfort with differences—can further influence how we treat others, often exacerbating these biases. Minorities are frequently on the receiving end of these biases and insecurities, which creates environments where they feel isolated, excluded, and undervalued.

SOLUTION:

a. **Reflect on Personal Biases and Insecurities:** It is essential to regularly self-reflect on how both unconscious biases and personal insecurities may influence our interactions and decisions. Tools like Harvard's Implicit Association Test (IAT) can help identify hidden biases, while personal reflection can help uncover insecurities that may affect how we relate to others. By becoming more aware of these influences, we can better address them in our daily lives. Additionally, seeking out diverse perspectives in our conversations and the media we consume helps us to become more understanding of other viewpoints, and ultimately more inclusive in our actions.

b. **Create Inclusive Spaces:** In social, professional, or community settings, make a deliberate effort to create opportunities for minority voices to be heard. If you observe someone being interrupted or overlooked, step in to ensure they have a chance to contribute. This action not only addresses bias but also helps overcome personal insecurities related to navigating diverse perspectives. It reinforces the value of inclusivity and ensures that diverse viewpoints are respected and heard.

3. SILENCE IN THE FACE OF INEQUITIES

Problem: Many people support the idea of EDI but feel uncertain about how to speak up when they witness inequities. This hesitation can lead to passivity, allowing microaggressions and exclusionary behaviors to persist unchallenged, thus perpetuating culture of silence, thus making minorities feel hopeless.

SOLUTION:

a. **Be an Active Advocate for Inclusion:** To foster more inclusive environments, it is essential to speak up when you witness microaggressions or discriminatory practices. Whether it's in a social circle, workplace, or community, practicing assertiveness in low-stakes situations helps build the confidence needed to address inequities in more significant moments.

b. **Seek Out EDI Education:** Education is key to building confidence in addressing inequities. By regularly attending EDI workshops, reading about diverse experiences, or participating in training programs, individuals and communities can gain the knowledge necessary to challenge discriminatory behaviors effectively.

4. MICROAGGRESSIONS AND THEIR IMPACT

Problem: Microaggressions, which are subtle yet harmful behaviors, often go unnoticed but can have a profound impact on the mental health and confidence of those who experience them. These behaviors may be difficult to address because they are not always overt or intentional, but their cumulative effect creates a hostile and isolating environment.

SOLUTION:

a. **Call Out Microaggressions Respectfully:** When you witness or experience a microaggression, address it respectfully by naming the behavior and explaining its impact. Using "I" statements (e.g., "I felt uncomfortable when...") can help de-escalate the situation and create an opportunity

for constructive dialogue. This approach allows the person to reflect on their actions without feeling attacked.
b. **Support Those Affected:** If you observe someone else experiencing a microaggression, act as an ally by acknowledging what happened and offering your support. This simple act of solidarity can have a powerful effect, reinforcing that the person's experience is valid and that they are not alone.

5. LACK OF CULTURAL AWARENESS FROM AN EARLY AGE

Problem: Many biases stem from a lack of exposure to diverse cultures and perspectives during formative years. Without early intervention, stereotypes and narrow viewpoints can become deeply ingrained, making them difficult to challenge in adulthood. As a society, we need to take responsibility for fostering cultural awareness from a young age.

SOLUTION:

a. **Encourage Cultural Conversations at Home:** Parents, educators, and community leaders should take the lead in promoting cultural awareness. By exposing children to different cultures, traditions, and perspectives early on, we can help them develop a more open-minded and inclusive worldview. Discussing diverse identities, experiences, and histories helps break down stereotypes and fosters empathy.
b. **Challenge Stereotypes:** When children (or adults) express stereotypical assumptions, use it as a teaching moment. Ask open-ended questions like, "Why do you think that's true?" or "Have you considered another perspective?" This encourages critical thinking and helps dismantle long-held stereotypes, leading to more thoughtful and inclusive attitudes in the future.

Final Thoughts: Building Empathy, One Step at a Time

The goal of this book was not just to inform but to spark real, lasting change in how we engage with one another. Equity, Diversity, and Inclusion (EDI) are not about grand gestures or waiting for sweeping transformations—they are built through small, deliberate actions that, together, create a ripple effect across our communities. I hope that by reading this book, you've been encouraged to see EDI not as an abstract concept but as a daily practice—one that you can champion in every interaction, big or small.

What minorities ask for is not special treatment or lower expectations—it's simply a bit of empathy and understanding. The systems and structures that many take for granted were built with certain assumptions and values in mind, and those values often do not include the perspectives or experiences of people like us. What we need is not sympathy, but an acknowledgement of the additional burdens we carry and a commitment to lightening that load by educating yourself and others. You have no idea how much it means that you've read this book this far. It shows that you care, that you are willing to engage with this difficult conversation, and that you want to be part of the change.

Through sharing personal stories, research, and practical strategies, I aimed to equip you with the tools to make a difference, starting from wherever you are. True inclusivity begins with empathy, respect, and the courage to challenge norms, no matter how uncomfortable it may feel. While individual steps may seem small, each action contributes to building a world where every voice is valued and every person feels a sense of belonging. If this book has resonated with you, share it. Gift it to a friend or colleague. Recommend it in meetings, seminars, or book clubs. Let this be the start of a conversation that helps others understand these realities, not just as abstract concepts, but as lived experiences.

Inclusion is built through collective action, empathy, and a willingness to be uncomfortable. Thank you for taking the time to reflect, learn, and start your journey toward greater understanding and advocacy. With your support, we can build a world where respect, empathy, and inclusivity are not just aspirations but the standard by which we all live and work.

Remember, real change is cumulative. Every choice you make—whether it's speaking up, listening deeply, or amplifying underrepresented voices—paves the way for broader societal shifts. It's in these intentional moments that we redefine what inclusion looks like and set the foundation for a more just world.

So don't wait for others to lead—be the leader in your space. Create opportunities, challenge inequities, and foster environments where everyone can thrive. Because meaningful change starts with us, right here, right now.

FINAL EXERCISE: YOUR PATH FORWARD

As you complete this book, take a moment to think about how the ideas and experiences shared can inspire change in your own life and community. Use the following prompts to guide your thoughts:

1. **How will you use what you've learned?**

    Reflect on how the concepts and personal stories in this book will influence your approach to equity, diversity, and inclusion. In what ways will you apply these insights to create a more inclusive environment in your workplace, social circle, or community?

    _____
    _____
    _____
    _____

2. **What challenges do you anticipate?**

    Consider the barriers you might face as you try to advocate for inclusivity or address inequities. How can you prepare yourself to overcome these obstacles, and who can you rely on for support?

    _____
    _____
    _____
    _____

3. **How will you hold yourself accountable?**

   It's easy to feel motivated after reading, but sustained change requires commitment. What steps will you take to ensure you hold yourself accountable in fostering inclusivity and confronting inequities over time?

   _____

   _____

   _____

4. **Who will you bring into this conversation?**

   Think about the people in your life—colleagues, friends, or family—who could benefit from understanding the importance of EDI. How will you initiate meaningful discussions about these topics with them?

   _____

   _____

   _____

By reflecting on these questions, you're setting the stage for taking meaningful, actionable steps toward creating a more equitable world. Congratulations on reaching this point and for taking the time to reflect on your role in fostering change. I'm deeply grateful for your commitment to this journey—your efforts matter, and together, we can build a more inclusive and understanding future.

REFERENCES

1. Amnesty International Canada. (2020). *Land Acknowledgements: Respecting the land and Indigenous peoples.* Amnesty International Canada. Retrieved from https://www.amnesty.ca

2. Banaji, M. R., & Greenwald, A. G. (2013). *Blindspot: Hidden biases of good people.* Delacorte Press.

3. Brown, B. (2018). *Dare to lead: Brave work. Tough conversations. Whole hearts.* Random House.

4. Canadian Human Rights Commission. (2016). *Employment equity and diversity in Canada.* Retrieved from https://www.chrc-ccdp.gc.ca

5. Canadian Museum of Immigration at Pier 21. (n.d.). *The evolution of Canadian immigration policy.* Retrieved from https://pier21.ca/research/immigration-history/the-evolution-of-canadian-immigration-policy

6. Catalyst. (2020). The power of inclusion in meetings. *Catalyst.* Retrieved from https://www.catalyst.org/research/the-power-of-inclusion-in-meetings/

7. CIPD. (2020). *Diversity and inclusion in the workplace: Creating a better workplace for everyone.* Retrieved from https://www.cipd.co.uk/knowledge/fundamentals/relations/diversity/factsheet

8. Community Solutions. (2019). *Why workplace diversity and inclusion matters.* Retrieved from https://www.communitysolutions.com

9. Deloitte. (2021). *The diversity and inclusion revolution: Eight powerful truths.* Deloitte Insights. Retrieved from https://

www2.deloitte.com/insights/us/en/focus/diversity-inclusion/redefining-diversity-and-inclusion.html

10. Edmondson, A. C. (1999). Psychological safety and learning behavior in work teams. Administrative Science Quarterly, 44(2), 350-383. https://doi.org/10.2307/2666999

11. Ferdman, B. M., & Sagiv, L. (2012). Cultural diversity in organizations: Theory, research, and practice. Oxford University Press.

12. Ferdman, B. M., & Sagiv, L. (2012). Diversity in organizations: A comprehensive guide to principles, practices, and policy. John Wiley & Sons.

13. Gap Inc. (n.d.). Diversity and inclusion: Our commitment to inclusion and belonging. Retrieved from https://www.gapinc.com/en-us/about/diversity-and-inclusion

14. Glossy. (n.d.). How Gap Inc. is pushing diversity initiatives through the Color Proud Council. Retrieved from https://www.glossy.co/diversity-and-inclusion/

15. Government of Canada. (2020). *Employment equity act*. Retrieved from https://laws-lois.justice.gc.ca/eng/acts/e-5.401/

16. Groysberg, B., & Connolly, K. (2013). Great leaders who make the mix work. *Harvard Business Review*. Retrieved from https://hbr.org/2013/09/great-leaders-who-make-the-mix-work

17. Gundling, E. (2016). What Western business leaders can learn from the Asian style of leadership. Harvard Business Review. Retrieved from https://hbr.org/2016/12/what-western-business-leaders-can-learn-from-the-asian-style-of-leadership

18. Gundling, E. (2016). Leading across new borders: How to succeed as the center shifts. Wiley.

19. Harris, A., McDonald, D., & Sparks, C. (2018). The impact of racial isolation and microaggressions on mental health among minority workers. Psychology Today. Retrieved from https://www.psychologytoday.com/us/blog/cultural-

ly-speaking/201807/the-impact-racial-isolation-and-micro-aggressions-mental-health

20. Harris, F. A., Palazzolo, A., & Sprague, R. (2018). The emotional labor of minority leadership. Journal of Leadership and Organizational Studies, 25(1), 30-45. https://doi.org/10.1177/1548051817745011

21. Harvard Gazette. (2021). *Understanding unconscious bias and its role in workplace diversity*. Retrieved from https://www.gazette.harvard.edu/unconscious-bias

22. Ivey Business School. (2018). *Data-driven strategies for diversity and inclusion in organizations*. Retrieved from https://www.ivey.uwo.ca/insight/

23. Ivey Business School. (2018). The role of unconscious bias in professional environments. Retrieved from https://www.ivey.uwo.ca/insight/2018/the-role-of-unconscious-bias-in-professional-environments/

24. Janis, I. L. (1982). *Groupthink: Psychological studies of policy decisions and fiascoes* (2nd ed.). Houghton Mifflin.

25. Kahneman, D. (2011). *Thinking, fast and slow*. Farrar, Straus and Giroux.

26. Knowledge at Wharton. (2018). *Starbucks' bold move: The lessons behind anti-bias training*. Retrieved from https://knowledge.wharton.upenn.edu/article/starbucks-bias-training/

27. Lev-Ari, S., & Keysar, B. (2010). Why don't we believe non-native speakers? The influence of accent on credibility. *Journal of Experimental Social Psychology, 46*(6), 1093-1096. https://doi.org/10.1016/j.jesp.2010.05.025

28. McGill University. (2020). *Land Acknowledgement and its role in fostering inclusivity*. Retrieved from https://www.mcgill.ca/landAcknowledgement

29. McKinsey & Company. (2020). *Diversity wins: How inclusion matters*. Retrieved from https://www.mckinsey.com/featured-insights/diversity-and-inclusion/diversity-wins-how-inclusion-matters

30. Miller, J. (2020). Insecurity and bias in the workplace: How threatened identities shape interactions. Harvard Business Review. Retrieved from https://hbr.org/2020/07/insecurity-and-bias-in-the-workplace

31. National Centre for Collaboration in Indigenous Education (NCCIE). (2019). *The importance of meaningful land Acknowledgements in Canada.* Retrieved from https://www.nccie.ca/land-Acknowledgement/

32. Psychology Today. (2018). The psychological toll of workplace microaggressions on minorities. Retrieved from https://www.psychologytoday.com/us/blog/culturally-speaking/201808/the-psychological-toll-workplace-microaggressions-minorities

33. SHRM. (2020). How diversity can drive innovation. SHRM. https://www.shrm.org/hr-today/news/hr-magazine/pages/0515-diversity.aspx

34. Stasiulis, D., & Bakan, A. B. (1997). *Negotiating citizenship: Migrant women in Canada and the global system.* University of Toronto Press.

35. Sue, D. W., Capodilupo, C. M., Torino, G. C., Bucceri, J. M., Holder, A. M. B., Nadal, K. L., & Esquilin, M. (2007). Racial microaggressions in everyday life: Implications for clinical practice. *American Psychologist, 62*(4), 271-286.

36. Scott, C. P., et al. (2020). Understanding the dynamics of microaggressions in professional settings. *Journal of Diversity in Organizations, 18*(3), 113-129. https://doi.org/10.1093/XXX

37. The Canadian Encyclopedia. (n.d.). *Employment equity and diversity in Canada.* Retrieved from https://www.thecanadianencyclopedia.ca

38. The Independent. (2019). *Why Black employees are more likely to leave their jobs due to lack of diversity.* Retrieved from https://www.independent.co.uk/news/diversity-workplace-black-employees

39. The Peak. (2021). *The deeper meaning of land Acknowledgements in Canada.* Retrieved from https://www.thepeak.ca/land-Acknowledgements-in-canada

40. Thomas, D. A., & Ely, R. J. (1996). Making differences matter: A new paradigm for managing diversity. Harvard Business Review, 74(5), 79-90. https://hbr.org/1996/09/making-differences-matter-a-new-paradigm-for-managing-diversity

41. Venkatesh, V. (2019). *Discriminatory immigration policies in Canada: A historical perspective. Journal of Canadian Studies*, 54(1), 44-68.

42. Williams, J. C., Li, S., Rincon, R., & Finn, P. (2016). "Prove it again" bias: A pervasive form of bias where women and minorities are held to higher standards. *Harvard Business Review.*

43. Workplace Communication. (2020). *The cost of feeling unheard: How employee voices shape retention.* Retrieved from https://www.workplacecommunication.com/employee-retention-voice/